Yes, I'm Divorced: So What!

The Journey Beyond The Ending

Author: Hulla Cooper

ISBN: 978-976-97377-0-9
First Edition: December 2024
Published by: Hulla Cooper
For permissions requests, please get in touch with the author at ula_milton@yahoo.com

DISCLAIMER

The information provided in this book is based on the author's personal experiences and research, including responses from real individuals who have participated in the research process. Every effort has been made to ensure the information's accuracy and completeness. However, the assume no responsibility for errors, inaccuracies, omissions, or inconsistencies.

The personal experiences shared in this book are the property of the individuals who provided them. These experiences have been included with their consent and anonymized to protect their privacy.

CREDITS

This book's information is derived from various online sources and journals. Full references for these sources can be found in the References section of this book.

Scripture References:
All scripture quotations are taken from the King James Version of the Bible, which is in the public domain.

DEDICATION

I dedicate this book to every resilient individual who has faced the challenges of divorce and chosen to overcome the pain. Your strength, resilience, and unyielding spirit are commendable. Within these pages, may you find hope, healing, and the promise of a brighter future filled with possibilities and joy.

I am deeply grateful to my three daughters, Sashe', Shoan, and Sahar, who have been more than just my unwavering pillars of strength throughout the aftermath of my 23-year marriage. Their love and support have been my rock, and I am deeply appreciative. I extend my heartfelt thanks to the friends who also offered steadfast support. Your encouragement has been invaluable in my writing journey.

To those who shared their personal stories and insights, thank you for your honesty and openness. Your experiences are the heart of this book; without your contributions, it is complete. May this book guide readers towards new beginnings rich with joy, purpose, and limitless possibilities.

CONTENTS

PREFACE

Yes **I am divorced: So What!** was born from my own journey through the stormy seas of divorce. Like many of you, I grappled with feelings of guilt, shame, uncertainty, disappointment, condemnation, and, most of all, a profound sense of loss and confusion.

I had surrendered my name and identity to become a wife at a tender age. Now, in the aftermath of divorce, I was left with a myriad of questions. What should I do with my life? Who am I now? What will my name be? Everyone knows me as Mrs. C. How do I transition from Mrs. C to ????, and more dauntingly, what will I transition to? It was during this tumultuous process that I recognized the need for a comprehensive guide to assist others in finding healing and renewal.

This book is a culmination of extensive research, heartfelt conversations, and the generous sharing of personal stories by brave individuals who have walked this path. Their experiences and insights form the backbone of this work, providing real-life examples of resilience and transformation.

Throughout the writing process, I drew inspiration from the timeless wisdom of the King James Bible, which offers profound guidance and comfort. Integrating these scriptures with practical advice and personal testimonies, I aim to create a resource that is both spiritually uplifting and practically useful.

I am deeply grateful to all who contributed their stories and insights and to my family and friends for their unwavering support. This book provides encouragement and empowerment for anyone facing the aftermath of divorce. Remember, this is not the end of your story but the beginning of a new and extraordinary chapter.

Thank you for embarking on this journey with me. May you find hope, healing, and the courage to embrace your new identity.

Hulla Cooper

INTRODUCTION

Divorce, a profound and challenging experience, often brings a mix of emotions. While it may be accompanied by sorrow and guilt, it also ushers in a sense of relief and hope. It signifies the end of one chapter but also the beginning of another, brimming with opportunities for personal growth, self-discovery, and new beginnings.

"Yes I am Divorced: So What!" is a guide crafted to support and encourage you through this transformative journey. Rooted in timeless wisdom from the King James Bible, this book not only aims to uplift your spirit and help you overcome feelings of guilt and condemnation but also to provide practical steps for rebuilding your life, all while offering spiritual support from biblical references.

The aftermath of a divorce can be a time of significant emotional upheaval. It's natural to feel a sense of loss and uncertainty about the future. However, this period can also be a time of tremendous personal growth and renewal. As it says in **Isaiah 43:18-19,** *"Remember ye, not the former things, neither consider the things of old. Behold, I will do a new thing; now it shall spring forth; shall ye not know it? I will even make a way in the wilderness and rivers in the desert."*

Yes, I'm Divorced: So What! seeks to empower you to embrace this new chapter with faith and confidence, knowing that a brighter future awaits.

Guilt and condemnation are common emotions after a divorce, often exacerbated by societal judgments or personal feelings of failure.

However, it is essential to understand that everyone makes mistakes, and God's grace is abundant. **Romans 8:1** reassures us, *"There is therefore now no condemnation to them which are in Christ Jesus, who walk not after the flesh, but after the Spirit."* By embracing this truth, you can release guilt and walk forward in freedom and forgiveness, feeling comforted and supported by God's grace.

Moving forward after a divorce involves practical and intentional steps. ***Yes, I'm Divorced: So What!*** is designed to guide you as you navigate through your situation and the various aspects of your new life. From managing finances and co-parenting to re-entering the dating scene and setting personal goals, each chapter offers actionable advice and biblical wisdom.

Proverbs 3:5-6 advises, *"Trust in the Lord with all thine heart; and lean not unto thine own understanding. In all thy ways acknowledge him, and he shall direct thy paths."* By trusting in God's guidance and the practical steps outlined in this book, you can confidently take steps towards rebuilding and enriching your life.

Chapter One:

ACCEPTANCE AND ACKNOWLEDGMENT

The dissolution of a marriage is a profound life event that can result in feelings of disorientation and being overwhelmed. The initial step in healing and reconstructing your life is recognising and accepting your new reality.

Accepting that your marriage has ended is not about assigning blame or reliving the past; it's about making peace with what has happened and understanding that a new chapter is beginning.

This new chapter is not a mere possibility, but a promise waiting to be fulfilled. You have the power to shape it, and you can make it a fulfilling one.

The Bible teaches us about the importance of acceptance and moving forward. **Ecclesiastes 3:1-4,** it states, *"To everything there is a season and a time to every purpose under the heaven: A time to be born, and a time to die; a time to plant, and a time to pluck up that which is planted; A time to kill, and a time to heal; a time to break down, and a time to build up; A time to weep, and a time to laugh; a time to mourn, and a time to dance."*

This passage reminds us that life is full of seasons, and each season has its purpose. Your divorce is a season of transition, and accepting it is the first step towards healing and rebuilding.

RECOGNIZING AND ACCEPTING EMOTION

Going through a divorce often brings a whirlwind of emotions—sadness, anger, fear, and confusion. Recognizing and accepting these feelings as part of the healing process is crucial. Suppressing emotions can lead to prolonged pain and can hinder your ability to move forward. Allow yourself to grieve the end of your marriage, as it is a natural and crucial part of the healing process.

In **Psalm 34:18,** we find comfort in the promise that *"The Lord is nigh unto them that are of a broken heart; and saveth such as be of a contrite spirit."* This verse assures us that God is close to those who are heartbroken, and He provides comfort and salvation in times of deep sorrow.

THE IMPORTANCE OF SELF-COMPASSION

As you navigate this challenging time, being kind to yourself is crucial. Be sure to show yourself the same compassion and understanding you would extend to a needy friend. Self-compassion involves acknowledging your pain without self-judgment and recognizing that suffering and personal setbacks are part of the shared human experience.

According to Dr Kristin Neff, a pioneer in self-compassion research, self-compassion comprises three main elements: self-kindness, common humanity, and mindfulness. Neff explains that *"self-compassion provides the same benefits as high self-esteem without its drawbacks: rather than emphasizing what makes us special and different from others, it emphasizes what makes us the same"* **(Neff, 2011).** This perspective helps you understand that you are not alone in your struggles and that being kind to yourself is a critical component of recovery.

FINDING STRENGTH IN FAITH

Amidst life's trials, faith stands as a steadfast source of strength and comfort. Trusting in God's plan can bring a sense of peace and hope. As **Jeremiah 29:11** assures us, *'For I know the thoughts that I think toward you, saith the Lord, thoughts of peace, and not of evil, to give you an expected end.'* This trust in God's plan, even when it's not immediately clear, promises a future brimming with hope and possibility.

Alongside scriptural support, the embrace of a community within your church or a support group can be a beacon of emotional support and practical advice. Engaging with others who have walked similar paths can dissolve the sense of isolation and foster a profound sense of understanding and empathy.

MOVING FORWARD WITH INTENTION

Acceptance is not a passive act but a deliberate step towards healing and rebuilding. By setting small, achievable goals for yourself, you can take control of this new chapter. Whether it's rekindling old hobbies, establishing a new routine, or seeking professional help, each step is a stride towards reclaiming your life and shaping a future that mirrors your true self.

In **Proverbs 3:5- 6**, we are advised to *"Trust in the Lord with all thine heart; and lean not unto thine own understanding. In all thy ways acknowledge him, and he shall direct thy paths."* By trusting God and taking intentional steps forward, you can navigate this difficult period with purpose and hope.

CONCLUSION

Acceptance and acknowledgement are the foundational steps towards healing after a divorce. Embrace the end of your marriage as the beginning of a new chapter, recognize and accept your emotions, practice self-compassion, find strength in your faith, and move forward with intention.

Remember that God is with you throughout this journey, offering comfort, guidance, and a hope-filled future.

Reflection Chapter One

Q1. Reflect on a time when you experienced a significant change. How did you cope with that change, and what positive outcomes eventually came from it?

Q2. What helps you feel comforted and supported when you feel heartbroken? Can you remember a recent moment when you felt God's presence?

Q3. Think about a moment recently when you were hard on yourself. What could you say to yourself instead to show more kindness and understanding?

Q4. Proverbs 3:5- 6 advises us to trust the Lord and not lean on our understanding. Are there any parts of your future that feel uncertain or scary right now? How might trusting God's plan help you feel more at peace about these areas?

Q5. What small goal can you set this week to make you feel more positive and proactive about your future? How will achieving this goal help you move forward?

Chapter Two:

LETTING GO OF GUILT AND SHAME

Divorce often brings a heavy burden of guilt and shame, emotions that are universally experienced. These feelings may arise from various sources, such as societal expectations, personal values, or the perception of failure in a significant life commitment. It's important to distinguish between guilt and shame: guilt is feeling remorse for actions taken, while shame is feeling bad about who you are. Both can be debilitating if not `appropriately addressed.

The Bible speaks to these feelings and offers pathways to release them. **Romans 3:23** reminds us, *"For all have sinned, and come short of the glory of God."* This verse acknowledges that imperfection is a universal human condition and that making mistakes is part of being human. However, it does not reflect one's worth or ability to lead a fulfilling life.

REFRAMING THE DIVORCE NARRATIVE

Reframing your divorce narrative is crucial for letting go of guilt and shame. Instead of viewing your divorce as a failure, consider it a learning experience and a step towards a healthier, more fulfilling life. Reflect on what you have learned about yourself and your needs and how this knowledge can guide you in the future.

Isaiah 43:18-19 offers a powerful perspective: *"Remember ye, not the former things, neither consider the things of old. Behold, I will do a new thing; now it shall spring forth; shall ye not know it? I will even make a way in the wilderness and rivers in the desert."*

This passage encourages you to release the past and embrace new opportunities.

STEPS TO RELEASE SELF-BLAME

Releasing oneself from self-blame requires a deliberate effort to practice self-forgiveness and move forward. Commence the process by openly acknowledging feelings of guilt and shame without engaging in self-judgment. Understand that these emotions are natural but do not define you.

According to Brené Brown, a research professor and expert on shame and vulnerability, self-compassion is vital to overcoming shame. In her work, Brown emphasizes the importance of speaking to yourself with kindness and understanding, as you would to a friend.

She writes, *"Shame corrodes the very part of us that believes we are capable of change"* **(Brown, 2012).** By practising self-compassion, you can begin to heal and build resilience.

SEEKING FORGIVENESS

Seeking forgiveness from others and yourself is vital in letting go of guilt and shame. This does not necessarily mean reconciling with your ex-spouse or seeking their approval, but rather finding peace within your heart.

1 **John 1:9 reassures** us, *"If we confess our sins, he is faithful and just to forgive us our sins, and to cleanse us from all unrighteousness."* Confession and seeking God's forgiveness can be a decisive step towards inner peace.

Remember that God's grace is boundless, and His forgiveness is a gift that allows you to start anew.

BUILDING A SUPPORT SYSTEM

Surrounding yourself with supportive, understanding people can help you navigate feelings of guilt and shame. Having a network of people who can offer encouragement and perspective, whether it's friends, family, or support groups, is invaluable.

Hebrews 10:24-25 encourages us to support one another: *"And let us consider one another to provoke unto love and to good works: Not forsaking the assembling of ourselves together, as the manner of some is; but exhorting one another: and so much the more, as ye see the day approaching."* Lean on your community and allow them to help you through this challenging time.

EMBRACING GOD'S GRACE

Finally, embracing God's grace is essential for letting go of guilt and shame. Accept that you are worthy of love and forgiveness, not because of what you have done, but because of who God is. His love and mercy are unconditional.

Ephesians 2:8-9 reminds us, *"For by grace are ye saved through faith; and that not of yourselves: it is the gift of God: Not of works, lest any man should boast."*

Accepting God's grace means understanding that you do not have to earn His love or forgiveness—it is freely given. This realization can liberate you from guilt and shame, allowing you to move forward with a renewed sense of purpose and self-worth.

CONCLUSION

Releasing oneself from feelings of guilt and shame following a divorce necessitates a journey marked by patience, self-compassion, and faith. By reframing your narrative, seeking forgiveness, building a support system, and embracing God's grace, you can release the heavy burdens that hold you back.

Remember that you are not alone in this journey; God's love and forgiveness are always available. As you move forward, let go of the past and embrace the new opportunities that await, confident in the knowledge that you are worthy of happiness and peace.

Reflection Chapter Two

Q1. Reflect on Romans 3:23, "For all have sinned, and come short of the glory of God." How does knowing that everyone makes mistakes help you forgive yourself for something related to your divorce?

Q2. Can you remember when someone else's understanding or support helped you feel less ashamed? How can you seek out more of that kind of support?

Q3. Reflect on Isaiah 43:18-19, "Remember ye, not the former things, neither consider the things of old. Behold, I will do a new thing." What lesson did you learn from that mistake, and how can you use it to improve your future?

Q4. When you feel overwhelmed by guilt or shame, what positive action can you take to remind yourself of God's love and forgiveness according to Proverbs 3:5-6?

Q5. What is one thing you can do this week to show kindness to yourself, especially when negative thoughts about your divorce arise?

Chapter Three:

REBUILDING YOUR SELF-WORTH

Divorce can often lead to a crisis of identity. When a marriage ends, it's common to feel like you've lost a part of yourself. The roles you play and your identity as part of a couple are no longer there, leaving you uncertain about who you are. Rediscovering your identity is a vital step in rebuilding your self-worth.

The Bible offers guidance on understanding your worth beyond earthly relationships. **Psalm 139:14** says, *"I will praise thee; for I am fearfully and wonderfully made: marvellous are thy works; and that my soul knoweth right well."* This verse reminds you that your worth is inherent and divinely ordained. You are incredibly unique, and your worth is not contingent upon your marital status.

EMBRACING SELF-CARE

Self-care is not just about pampering yourself; it is about taking deliberate actions to improve your physical, emotional, and mental well-being. After a divorce, prioritizing self-care is crucial for rebuilding your self-worth. This can include activities that nourish your body, mind, and spirit.

Engage in activities that make you feel good and help you connect with yourself. Whether exercising, reading, meditating, or spending time in nature, find what makes you feel alive and reconnected with your true self.

Remember **1 Corinthians 6:19-20**, which teaches, *"What? Know Ye not that your body is the temple of the Holy Ghost, which is in you, which ye have of God, and you are not your own? For ye are bought with a price: therefore, glorify God in your body, and in your spirit, which is God's."* Caring for your body and spirit honours God and reinforces your intrinsic value.

SETTING BOUNDARIES

Establishing robust boundaries is a fundamental aspect of nurturing one's self-worth. These boundaries play a pivotal role in safeguarding one's emotional and mental well-being by unequivocally delineating acceptable conduct within personal relationships and interactions. They empower you to take control of your life and ensure your needs are met.

Reflect on the importance of boundaries in **Proverbs 4:23**, *"Keep thy heart with all diligence; for out of it are the issues of life."* Guarding your heart involves setting limits that prevent others from taking advantage of you or diminishing your sense of self-worth. Establishing and upholding boundaries signifies an individual's self-esteem and self-care.

PURSUING PERSONAL GROWTH

Personal growth is an ongoing journey throughout life. After a divorce, pursuing personal growth can help you rediscover a sense of purpose and direction. This involves setting new goals, learning new skills, and exploring new interests. By focusing on your development, you can rebuild your self-esteem and discover new passions.

Philippians 4:13 encourages, *"I can do all things through Christ which strengtheneth me."* With this mindset, approach new challenges and opportunities with confidence. Whether you decide to take up a new hobby, advance your career, or further your education, trust that you have the strength and ability to succeed.

CONNECTING WITH OTHERS

Reconstructing one's self-worth necessitates establishing meaningful connections with others. Surround yourself with supportive, positive individuals who uplift and encourage you. Engage in activities that facilitate the establishment of new acquaintances and the forging of fresh friendships. Cultivating a robust social network can furnish emotional sustenance and augment your sense of belonging.

Hebrews 10:24-25 advises, *"And let us consider one another to provoke unto love and to good works: Not forsaking the assembling of ourselves together, as the manner of some is; but exhorting one another: and so much the more, as ye see the day approaching."* Engaging with a community and fostering positive relationships can help you feel supported and valued.

CONCLUSION

Rebuilding your self-worth after a divorce is a multifaceted process that involves rediscovering your identity, embracing self-care, setting boundaries, pursuing personal growth, and connecting with others.

By focusing on these areas and drawing strength from your faith, you can reclaim your sense of self and move forward with confidence and resilience. Remember that your worth is inherent and divinely given, and you can build a fulfilling and meaningful life.

Reflection Chapter Three

Q1. Think about things you love about yourself. What are some qualities or talents you possess that you can celebrate?

Q2. What are some activities that make you feel good and valued? How can you make time for these activities in your daily routine?

Q3. Reflect on Proverbs 4:23, "Keep thy heart with all diligence." What boundaries must you set to protect your emotional and mental health?

Q4. What new hobbies or interests would you like to try that can help you grow as a person?

Q5. Who are the supportive people in your life that make you feel good about yourself? How can you spend more time with them to feel more connected and valued?

Chapter Four:

HEALING EMOTIONALLY

Divorce brings about a unique type of grief, as it involves the loss of a significant relationship and the dreams that come with it. This grief can be profound and multifaceted, encompassing sadness, anger, confusion, and even relief. It's important to understand that these emotions are valid, and embracing the grieving process is crucial for emotional healing.

The Bible acknowledges the depth of human sorrow and offers comfort. In **Psalm 147:3,** it is written, *"He healeth the broken in heart, and bindeth up their wounds."* This verse reminds us that God is close to hurting people and provides healing for their wounds. Accepting your grief and allowing yourself to mourn is a vital step towards recovery, knowing that you are not alone in this journey.

FINDING CLOSURE

Finding closure after a divorce can be challenging, especially when there are unresolved issues or lingering emotions. However, closure doesn't mean erasing the past; it means coming to terms with it and finding peace. This process empowers you to reflect on the marriage, acknowledge both the positive and negative aspects, and understand that the end of the relationship doesn't diminish your worth or prospects.

In **Ecclesiastes 3:1**, we are reminded, *"To everything there is a season, and a time to every purpose under the heaven."* This passage teaches us that life is full of seasons, each with its purpose. Accepting that the season of your marriage has ended can help you find closure and move forward.

EMOTIONAL SELF-CARE

Emotional self-care involves actively nurturing one's emotional well-being. This can include journaling one's thoughts and feelings, seeking therapy or counselling, and engaging in activities that bring joy and peace. It also means being patient with oneself and allowing time for healing.

Philippians 4:6-7 offers reassurance: *"Be careful for nothing; but in everything by prayer and supplication with thanksgiving let your requests be made known unto God. And the peace of God, which passeth all understanding, shall keep your hearts and minds through Christ Jesus."* Turning to prayer and meditation can provide immense comfort and help maintain emotional balance.

RELEASING ANGER AND BITTERNESS

Divorce can leave you with feelings of anger and bitterness, especially if the separation involves betrayal or deep hurt. Holding onto these emotions can hinder your healing process and affect your future relationships. Releasing anger and bitterness is crucial for your emotional well-being.

Ephesians 4:31-32 advises, *"Let all bitterness, and wrath, and anger, and clamour, and evil speaking, be put away from you, with all malice: And be ye kind one to another, tenderhearted, forgiving one another, even as God for Christ's sake hath forgiven you."* Even if it's challenging, practising forgiveness can free you from anger and bitterness, paving the way for inner peace.

FINDING SUPPORT

Seeking support from friends, family, or support groups is crucial for emotional recovery. Sharing your experiences with individuals who empathize can offer solace and valuable perspective. Additionally, it can alleviate feelings of isolation and foster a sense of interconnectedness.

Proverbs 17:17 reminds us, *"A friend loveth at all times, and a brother is born for adversity."* During adversity, seeking solace in the support of loved ones is advisable. Their unwavering encouragement can serve as a pillar of strength as you navigate through the complexities of your emotions.

BUILDING NEW ROUTINES

Establishing new routines can be instrumental in restoring a sense of normalcy and command in one's life. Forming daily practices that foster well-being, such as consistent exercise, nutritious eating, and ample rest, can significantly enhance one's emotional well-being. Participation in activities that bring enjoyment and a sense of fulfilment can also elevate mood and impart a sense of purpose.

In **Lamentations 3:22-23**, we find hope: *"It is of the Lord's mercies that we are not consumed, because his compassions fail not. They are new every morning: great is thy faithfulness."* Embracing the idea that each day is a new beginning filled with fresh opportunities can help you develop positive routines and move forward.

CONCLUSION

Healing emotionally after a divorce is a complex and ongoing process that requires embracing your grief, finding closure, practicing emotional self-care, releasing anger and bitterness, seeking support, and building new routines.

Remember that God's healing and comfort are always available to you. By leaning on your faith and taking intentional steps towards emotional well-being, you can navigate this challenging time and emerge stronger, more resilient, and ready to embrace the future.

Reflection Chapter Four

Q1. Reflect on Psalm 147:3, "He healeth the broken in heart, and bindeth up their wounds." How can you allow yourself to feel and process your grief healthily?

Q2. Consider a time when you found closure in a problematic situation. What helped you find peace, and how can you apply that to your divorce?

Q3. What activities or practices help you feel emotionally balanced and cared for? How can you include these in your daily life?

Q4. Ephesians 4:31-32 advises us to let go of anger and bitterness. What steps can you take to release any lingering anger or resentment?

Q5. Who are the people in your life who offer you support and understanding? How can you reach out to them more during this time?

Chapter Five:

MANAGING PRACTICAL MATTERS

Achieving financial independence is one of the most immediate and daunting challenges after a divorce. Adjusting to a single-income household can take time, whether you previously relied on a spouse's income or shared expenses. Taking stock of your financial situation and creating a plan to ensure stability and growth is essential.

Proverbs 21:5 says, *"The thoughts of the diligent tend only to plenteousness; but of everyone that is hasty only to want."* The passage above underscores the significance of meticulous planning and steadfastness in managing financial matters.

By formulating a comprehensive budget delineating your earnings, expenditures, and economic aspirations, you gain a sense of control over your financial future. Accord precedence to fundamental requirements such as accommodations, utilities, and sustenance, and endeavour to identify opportunities for curtailing discretionary outlays.

LEGAL CONSIDERATIONS

Divorce often involves various legal matters, including the division of assets, custody arrangements, and updating legal documents. It is crucial to understand your rights and responsibilities during this process clearly.

Seeking guidance from a qualified attorney can offer clarity and protect your interests. Additionally, updating indispensable documents such as your will, power of attorney, and beneficiary designations is advisable to align with your current circumstances.

Failure to update these documents can lead to unintended consequences, as they may still reflect your previous marital status. **Proverbs 11:14** reminds us, *"Where no counsel is, the people fall: but in the multitude of counsellors there is safety."* Relying on professional guidance can help you navigate the legal complexities of divorce.

HOUSING AND LIVING ARRANGEMENTS

Determining your housing and living arrangements is another significant aspect of managing practical matters. Whether you stay in your current home or move to a new place, choosing a living situation that supports your emotional and financial well-being is essential.

It is essential to thoroughly evaluate your options and carefully deliberate on choices that align with your needs and those of any children involved. **Philippians 4:19** provides reassurance: *"But my God shall supply all your need according to his riches in glory by Christ Jesus."* Trust that your needs will be met as you decide your living arrangements.

ORGANIZING AND DECLUTTERING

Divorce often requires reorganizing and decluttering your living space. This process can be therapeutic and symbolic of letting go of the past and making room for new beginnings. Start by meticulously categorizing your possessions and deciding what to retain, contribute, or eliminate. Dedicate your efforts to cultivating a welcoming environment that mirrors your style and inclinations.

Ecclesiastes 3:6 reminds us, *"A time to get, and a time to lose; a time to keep, and a time to cast away."* Embrace this time of transition as an opportunity to simplify and reorganize your life.

DEVELOPING A ROUTINE

Establishing a new daily regimen can engender a feeling of stability and regularity amid this period of change. A consistent routine helps manage time effectively and addresses important tasks and self-care activities. As you develop and stick to your routine, you'll feel a sense of accomplishment and control over your life.

1 Corinthians 14:40 advises, *"Let all things be done decently and in order."* Developing a well-structured daily routine can effectively mitigate stress and uphold organization in one's life.

SEEKING PROFESSIONAL HELP

Managing practical matters following a divorce can be daunting; however, seeking professional assistance can yield significant benefits. Financial advisors, legal professionals, and counsellors have the expertise to offer valuable support as you navigate these challenges. Their guidance can provide reassurance and a sense of support during this difficult time.

Proverbs 15:22 states, *"Without counsel purposes are disappointed: but in the multitude of counsellors they are established."* Engaging with professionals can help you make informed decisions and achieve your goals more effectively.

CONCLUSION

When navigating the practical implications of a divorce, it is essential to prioritize achieving financial independence, attending to legal considerations, establishing housing arrangements, organizing living spaces, creating structured routines, and seeking guidance from professional resources.

By approaching these tasks with diligence and relying on both faith and practical support, you can make a stable and secure foundation for your new life. Remember that faith can provide comfort and strength and guide your decisions and actions during this challenging time. God is with you in every step, giving guidance and strength as you navigate this difficult time.

Reflection Chapter Five

Q1. Think about your current financial situation. What steps can you take to create a budget that helps you feel more in control of your finances?

Q2. Reflect on Proverbs 11:14, "Where no counsel is, the people fall." How can seeking advice from a lawyer or financial advisor help you feel more secure about your future?

Q3. What are your housing needs right now? Would staying where you are or moving to a new place better support your well-being?

Q4. Consider Ecclesiastes 3:6, "A time to keep, and a time to cast away." How can decluttering and reorganizing your living space help you feel more at peace?

Q5. What new daily routines can you establish to help bring more order and stability to your life? How might these routines make your days feel more manageable?

Chapter Six:

PARENTING POST-DIVORCE

Parenting after a divorce can be one of the most challenging aspects of your new life. Co-parenting requires cooperation, communication, and a commitment to putting your children's needs first. Establishing a respectful and cooperative relationship with your ex-spouse is essential for the sake of your children. This can be achieved by setting clear boundaries, maintaining open communication, and focusing on the shared goal of providing the best for your children.

Ephesians 4:2-3 reminds us, *"With all lowliness and meekness, with longsuffering, forbearing one another in love; Endeavouring to keep the unity of the Spirit in the bond of peace."*

Strive to approach co-parenting with humility, patience, and a focus on unity and peace. Set clear, consistent guidelines for communication and decision-making, and always prioritize the well-being of your children.

HELPING CHILDREN ADJUST

The divorce of their parents can be an incredibly challenging experience for children. They might grapple with feelings of confusion, anxiety, and a sense of responsibility for the breakdown of their family unit. Providing them with ongoing reassurance, stability, and a safe environment to express their emotions openly is crucial in helping them navigate this difficult time.

Proverbs 22:6 says, *"Train up a child in the way he should go: and when he is old, he will not depart from it."* your children through this challenging time with love and wisdom will help them develop resilience and a sense of security. Create an environment where open and honest conversations are welcomed. Take the time to listen to their worries and fears genuinely. Through your words and actions, let them know they are loved and supported.

MAINTAINING FAMILY STABILITY

Creating a stable environment for your children involves maintaining routines and consistency as much as possible. For instance, regular meals, homework, and bedtime schedules provide a sense of normalcy and security.

Celebrating family traditions and creating new ones, such as a weekly family game night or a monthly movie marathon, is important to foster a sense of togetherness and continuity.

Psalm 127:3-4 reminds us, *"Lo, children are an heritage of the Lord: and the fruit of the womb is his reward. As arrows are in the hand of a mighty man, so are children of the youth."* Cherish your children as precious gifts and strive to provide them with a nurturing and stable home environment.

MANAGING YOUR OWN EMOTIONS

As a parent, managing your emotions effectively to support your children is essential. Children are perceptive and can pick up on your feelings of stress, anger, or sadness. Prioritizing your emotional well-being is crucial for becoming a more resilient and engaged parent. This can be achieved by practising self-care, seeking professional help, and finding a healthy outlet for your emotions.

Philippians 4:6-7 offers guidance: *"Be careful for nothing; but in everything by prayer and supplication with thanksgiving let your requests be made known unto God. And the peace of God, which passeth all understanding, shall keep your hearts and minds through Christ Jesus."* Turn to prayer and self-care practices to maintain your emotional balance and peace.

BUILDING A SUPPORT NETWORK

Building a support network of family, friends, and professionals can provide invaluable assistance and encouragement as you navigate parenting post-divorce. Surround yourself with individuals who comprehend your circumstances and can offer tangible emotional aid and reinforcement.

Ecclesiastes 4:9-10 emphasizes the importance of companionship: *"Two are better than one; because they have a good reward for their labour. For if they fall, the one will lift up his fellow: but woe to him that is alone when he falleth; for he hath not another to help him up."*
Rely on your support network to help you through the challenges of single parenting.

EMBRACING NEW FAMILY DYNAMICS

Divorce changes the dynamics of your family, and it's important to embrace these changes positively. Foster strong, individual relationships with your children and create an atmosphere of love and respect in your home. Focus on the new possibilities and opportunities this new phase of life brings.

In Isaiah 43:18-19, we are encouraged to look forward: *"Remember ye, not the former things, neither consider the things of old. Behold, I will do a new thing; now it shall spring forth; shall ye not know it? I will even make a way in the wilderness and rivers in the desert."* Embrace the new chapter of your family life with hope and optimism.

CONCLUSION

Navigating the journey of parenting post-divorce requires a thoughtful and strategic approach. It involves actively engaging in co-parenting discussions, being empathetic and supportive to help children adapt to the changes, ensuring stability within the family unit, managing and processing personal emotions, establishing a solid support system, and embracing the evolving dynamics of a restructured family. It's crucial to approach these challenges with a compassionate, patient, and faith-driven mindset to cultivate a nurturing and encouraging environment for your children.

Remember, you can always seek guidance and strength from your faith to guide you through this transformative journey.

Reflection Chapter Six

Q1. How can you improve communication with your ex-spouse to make co-parenting smoother for your children?

Q2. Reflect on Proverbs 22:6, "Train up a child in the way he should go." How can you provide reassurance and stability for your children during this time?

Q3. What routines or traditions can you maintain or create to help your children feel secure and connected?

Q4. Philippians 4:6-7 encourages finding peace through prayer. What self-care practices can you use to manage your emotions and stay balanced?

Q5. Who are the supportive people you can rely on for help and encouragement in your life? How can you involve them more in your journey of single parenting?

Chapter Seven:

REDEFINING RELATIONSHIPS

Divorce often brings significant changes to your social circles. Friends and family may react in various ways, and some relationships may become strained or dissolve. It is crucial to navigate these changes with grace and wisdom. Accept that some friendships may shift, but also recognize the exciting opportunity to forge new connections and strengthen existing ones that are supportive.

Proverbs 18:24 reminds us, *"A man that hath friends must shew himself friendly: and there is a friend that sticketh closer than a brother.* "Focus on nurturing relationships with those who provide genuine support and understanding. Seek out friends who can offer a listening ear and empathetic heart as you transition into this new phase of your life.Their support is invaluable and will make you feel valued and understood. Look for friends who are good listeners, empathetic, and non-judgmental. These are the qualities that will help you feel supported and understood during this challenging time.

REBUILDING TRUST

Rebuilding trust in yourself and others can be daunting after a divorce. Trust might have been broken during your marriage, leaving you vulnerable and cautious. Taking the time you need to heal and approach new relationships with an open yet discerning heart is essential.

Psalm 37:3 advises, *"Trust in the Lord, and do good; so shalt thou dwell in the land, and verily thou shalt be fed."* Trusting in God can provide security and peace as you rebuild trust in human relationships. Allow yourself to move forward at your own pace, knowing it's okay to be cautious and open to new connections. Remember, God is with you, offering guidance and comfort as you rebuild trust.

SETTING BOUNDARIES

Establishing healthy boundaries is crucial in all relationships, especially after a divorce. Boundaries help protect your emotional well-being and ensure respectful and supportive interactions with others. This might mean limiting contact with your ex-spouse to necessary co-parenting discussions or gently distancing yourself from friends not supportive of your new path.

Matthew 5:37 teaches, *"But let your communication be, Yea, yea; Nay, nay: for whatsoever is more than these cometh of evil."* Clear and honest communication about your needs and limits is essential in setting effective boundaries. Choosing to communicate directly and assertively can cultivate more robust, constructive relationships and promote a culture of respect and support in all interactions.

SEEKING NEW CONNECTIONS

Divorce can provide opportunities to seek new connections and build a social network that aligns more closely with your current values and interests. Joining community groups, clubs, or classes can help you meet new people who share your hobbies and passions. Volunteering is a fantastic opportunity to connect with like-minded individuals while making a meaningful impact on a cause you are passionate about.

Hebrews 10:24-25 encourages us to foster community: *"And let us consider one another to provoke unto love and to good works: Not forsaking the assembling of ourselves together, as the manner of some is; but exhorting one another: and so much the more, as ye see the day approaching."* Engaging with new communities can bring a profound sense of belonging and support as you redefine your social landscape.

EMBRACING SOLITUDE

While building new relationships is important, it's also crucial to recognize the value of embracing solitude as part of your healing process. Solitude is not about being alone, but about being comfortable with yourself and your thoughts. It allows self-reflection, personal growth, and a deeper connection with God. It provides the space to rediscover who you are outside of a relationship and to develop a stronger sense of independence and self-reliance, which are essential for your personal growth.

Isaiah 30:15 offers wisdom on the value of solitude: *"For thus saith the Lord God, the Holy One of Israel; In returning and rest shall ye be saved; in quietness and confidence shall be your strength."* Embrace moments of quiet and use them to reconnect with your inner self and your faith

STRENGTHENING FAMILY BONDS

Divorce affects your relationship with your ex-spouse and can also impact your extended family dynamics. Strengthening bonds with your family can provide a support system and a sense of continuity.

Spend quality time with supportive family members and involve them in your and your children's lives as much as possible. This could mean inviting them to school events, family dinners, or even regular phone calls to keep them updated on your and your children's lives.

Romans 12:10 encourages, "*Be kindly affectioned one to another with brotherly love; in honour preferring one another.*" By fostering loving and respectful relationships within your family, you create a solid foundation of support that can help you through this transitional period.

CONCLUSION

Redefining relationships after divorce involves navigating changes in social circles, rebuilding trust, setting boundaries, seeking new connections, embracing solitude, and strengthening family bonds. Each step is essential for creating a supportive and fulfilling social environment. Remember that God is with you every step of the way, offering His unwavering guidance and comfort as you rebuild and redefine your relationships.

Reflection Chapter Seven

Q1. Proverbs 18:24 talks about having friends that stick closer than a brother. How can you identify and nurture relationships with friends who provide genuine support and understanding during this transition?

Q2. What steps can you take to rebuild trust in yourself and others? How does trusting in God help you in this process?

Q3. What boundaries do you need to set in your relationships to protect your emotional well-being? How can you communicate these boundaries effectively?

Q4. What new activities or groups can you join to meet people who share your interests and values? How can these new connections support your personal growth?

Q5. How can you use moments of solitude to reconnect with yourself and your faith? What activities can help you embrace and enjoy your alone time?

Chapter Eight:

EMBRACING NEW OPPORTUNITIES

The dissolution of a marriage can catalyze self-discovery. It offers individuals the opportunity to engage in new interests and hobbies that may have been previously overlooked due to time constraints. This transitional period presents a prospect for self-redefinition and exploring pursuits that yield joy and fulfilment.

Ecclesiastes 3:1 is written, *"To everything, there is a season, and a time to every purpose under the heaven."* Embrace this season of your life as a time to explore and engage in exciting activities. Whether taking up a new sport, learning a musical instrument, or pursuing artistic endeavours, finding new interests can rejuvenate your spirit and open up new possibilities.

PURSUING EDUCATION AND CAREER GOALS

A significant aspect of embracing new opportunities is the potential for growth in your education and career. This might be the perfect time to pursue further education, acquire new skills, or make a career change. Investing in your professional development can lead to increased confidence and new opportunities.

Proverbs 24:14 encourages us, *"So shall the knowledge of wisdom be unto thy soul: when thou hast found it, there shall be a reward, and thy expectation shall not bc cut off.* Seek knowledge and skills that align with your passions and career aspirations. Whether through formal education or self-directed learning, advancing your career can bring a sense of accomplishment and purpose.

BUILDING NEW RELATIONSHIPS

While it's essential to take time to heal after a divorce, embracing new relationships can also be a part of your journey. New friendships and romantic relationships can provide companionship, support, and joy. Approach new relationships with an open heart and a clear understanding of what you need and want.

Song of Solomon 8:7 reflects the power of love, *"Many waters cannot quench love, neither can the floods drown it."* When you feel ready, be open to love and companionship again. Building new relationships can enrich your life and provide a supportive network as you move forward.

VOLUNTEERING AND GIVING BACK

Volunteering can be a fulfilling way to embrace new opportunities and give back to your community. Helping others not only makes a positive impact on those in need but also fosters a sense of purpose and connection.

Matthew 25:40 reminds us, *"And the King shall answer and say unto them, Verily I say unto you since ye have done it unto one of the least of these my brethren, ye have done it unto me."* By giving your time and energy to volunteer work, you can make meaningful contributions and find fulfilment in service.

FOCUSING ON HEALTH AND WELLNESS

Embracing new opportunities also involves prioritizing your health and wellness. This is an excellent time to establish healthy habits and routines to improve your physical, mental, and emotional well-being. Regular exercise, a balanced diet, and mindfulness practices can all contribute to a healthier, more vibrant life.

1 Corinthians 6:19-20 teaches, *"What? "now ye not that your body is the temple of the Holy Ghost which is in you, which ye have of God, and ye are not your own? For ye are bought with a price: therefore glorify God in your body, and in your spirit, which are God's.* God's care of your body and mind is essential to embracing new opportunities and living a fulfilling life.

TRAVELING AND EXPERIENCING NEW CULTURES

Travelling can be a transformative experience, offering new perspectives and enriching your understanding of the world. Exploring new places and experiencing different cultures can be an exciting way to embrace your newfound independence and curiosity.

Psalm 121:8 provides reassurance for your journeys, *"The Lord shall preserve thy going out and thy coming in from this time forth, and even for evermore."* Travelling can help you gain fresh insights, build confidence, and create lasting memories.

CONCLUSION

Harnessing the potential for personal growth post-divorce involves delving into new passions, pursuing educational and professional aspirations, cultivating fresh connections, engaging in community service, prioritizing physical and mental well-being, and immersing oneself in diverse cultural experiences through travel. By reimagining this phase as an opportunity for self-discovery and expansion, individuals can carve out a glorious and satisfying new chapter in their lives.

It's essential to remember that a guiding force is present throughout this journey, ushering individuals towards fresh prospects and abundant blessings. Embracing new opportunities after a divorce involves discovering new interests, pursuing education and career goals, building new relationships, volunteering, focusing on health and wellness, and experiencing new cultures through travel. By viewing this period as a time of growth and exploration, you can create a vibrant and fulfilling new chapter in your life.

Remember that God is with you every step of the way, guiding you towards new opportunities and blessings.

Reflection Chapter Eight

Q1. What new hobbies or interests have you considered exploring?

Q2. What educational or career goals could represent a new beginning in your life?

Q3. How can building new relationships help you embrace this new chapter in your life?

Q4. How can volunteering or helping others bring a new purpose to your life?

Q5. What health and wellness changes can you improve your overall well-being?

Chapter Nine:

THE CHURCH'S ROLE IN SUPPORTING STRUGGLING MARRIAGES

The church should be a supportive and guiding haven for its members, especially during tough times. Regrettably, some couples facing marital issues feel neglected or unsupported by their church community. This chapter delves into the significance of the church's role in offering assistance and resources to couples dealing with marital challenges.

THE CALL TO COMPASSION

In **Galatians 6:2** , we are instructed to *"Bear ye one another's burdens, and so fulfil the law of Christ."* The church serves as a place where a close-knit community of believers comes together to provide unwavering support for one another during challenging times. When couples confront marriage difficulties, the church extends compassion and assistance, offering a safe space for open dialogue, heartfelt prayers, and practical support to help navigate troubled waters.

RECOGNIZING THE SIGNS

A responsibility and a way to show care; in many instances, couples may endure their difficulties in silence, often out of shame or fear of judgment.

The church must cultivate an environment where members feel comfortable sharing their marital struggles without fearing condemnation. Both leaders and members should be vigilant and empathetic to any signs that indicate marital distress, such as sudden withdrawal from church activities, noticeable changes in behaviour, or manifestations of visible stress and unhappiness. Recognizing these signs is a responsibility and a way to show care and concern for our fellow members.

PROVIDING PRACTICAL HELP

James 2:15-16 says, *"If a brother or sister be naked, and destitute of daily food, And one of you say unto them, Depart in peace, be ye warmed and filled; not with standing ye give them not those things which are needful to the body; what doth it profit?"*

The church should not only offer spiritual support but also practical help. This can include marriage counseling services, support groups, and educational communication and conflict resolution workshops. This comprehensive support empowers couples to navigate their challenges with confidence and assurance.

ENCOURAGING OPEN DIALOGUE

Fostering an environment of openness and transparency encourages couples to seek the help they need. Churches can facilitate small group discussions, marriage retreats, and seminars that address common marital issues. By normalizing these conversations, couples will be more likely to seek support early on, preventing problems from escalating.

TRAINING CHURCH LEADERS

Church leaders should be equipped with the necessary skills to support couples effectively. This can include training in pastoral counselling, understanding the dynamics of marriage, and knowing when to refer couples to professional counsellors.

Church leaders should also proactively reach out to couples they suspect might face challenges, offering a listening ear and guidance. By being well-prepared and active, church leaders can offer meaningful and informed support, providing reassurance and confidence to the couples they serve.

PRAYING FOR MARRIAGES

The power of prayer should never be underestimated. 1 **Thessalonians 5:17** encourages us to *"Pray without ceasing."*

Churches can organize prayer groups dedicated to praying for marriages within the congregation. This provides spiritual support and fosters community and solidarity among members.

CONCLUSION

The church has a vital role in supporting couples facing marital challenges. By providing compassion, practical help, and a safe environment for open dialogue, the church can help strengthen marriages and prevent unnecessary breakdowns. Through fulfilling this role, the church embodies the love and support Christ calls us to show one another.

Reflection Chapter Nine

Q1. How can the church create a more supportive environment for couples facing marital challenges?

Q2. In what ways can church leaders be better trained to identify and address the needs of struggling couples?

Q3. How can open dialogue about marital issues without fear of judgment or condemnation be encouraged in the church?

Q4. What practical resources (e.g., counseling, support groups) can churches provide to help couples strengthen their marriages and avoid divorce?

Q5. Has the church done enough to help you navigate the challenges you faced during your marriage or separation?

Chapter Ten:
EMBRACING A NEW IDENTITY

Rediscovering your identity after a divorce is not just a challenge, but a journey of liberation. It's an opportunity to reconnect with who you are outside the context of a relationship, a journey that brings a profound sense of freedom and self-discovery. This process involves introspection and the willingness to explore new facets of yourself.

Jeremiah 29:11 is written, *"For I know the thoughts that I think toward you, saith the Lord, thoughts of peace, and not of evil, to give you an expected end."* This verse reassures us that God has a plan for our lives, one that is filled with hope and future possibilities.. Embracing a new identity means trusting this divine plan and allowing yourself to grow and evolve.

EXPLORING PERSONAL INTERESTS AND PASSIONS

One practical approach to embracing a new identity involves exploring personal interests and passions that may have been previously overlooked. Whether pursuing a hobby, engaging in travel, or acquiring new knowledge, active participation in activities that bring joy and satisfaction is not just essential, but also inspiring for fostering personal growth and attaining fulfillment.

A study in the Journal of Happiness Studies, authored by **Seligman (2002),** emphasizes that involvement in activities aligned with personal interests markedly enhances life satisfaction and overall well-being. By allocating time to endeavours that resonate personally, individuals can uncover new dimensions of themselves and foster a more prosperous, gratifying existence.

STRENGTHENING YOUR FAITH

For many, strengthening faith is not just essential, but a comforting anchor in the process of embracing a new identity. Reconnecting with your spiritual beliefs can provide comfort, guidance, and a sense of purpose during this transitional period, offering a reassuring anchor in times of change.

Isaiah 40:31 offers encouragement: *"But they that wait upon the Lord shall renew their strength; they shall mount up with wings as eagles; they shall run, and not be weary; and they shall walk, and not faint."* This verse highlights the rejuvenating power of faith and trust in God. Strengthening your faith can help you find peace and resilience as you navigate your new path.

BUILDING SELF-CONFIDENCE

Building self-confidence is a crucial aspect of embracing a new identity. Divorce can sometimes lead to self-doubt and a diminished sense of self-worth. However, setting small, achievable goals and celebrating accomplishments can rebuild confidence and self-esteem and provide encouragement and motivation.

Philippians 4:13 reminds us, *"I can do all things through Christ which strengtheneth me."* This verse powerfully reminds us of the strength and confidence we can find through faith. By directing attention to your strengths and accomplishments, you can foster a more positive self-perception and a more defined sense of self.

CONNECTING WITH A SUPPORTIVE COMMUNITY

Immersing oneself within a supportive community is not just a pivotal step but a crucial one towards fostering personal growth and shaping one's identity. Interacting with like-minded individuals with similar values and interests can offer encouragement and a profound sense of belonging and connection, making you feel understood and supported.

Proverbs 27:17 states, *"Iron sharpeneth iron; so a man sharpeneth the countenance of his friend."* This verse underscores the importance of supportive relationships in personal development. By actively seeking and nurturing these connections, you can enhance your journey of self-discovery.

EMBRACING CHANGE AND UNCERTAINTY

Embracing a new identity is akin to navigating uncharted waters, where change and uncertainty intertwine. Although this journey may seem formidable at first glance, it is also a profound opportunity for personal growth and meaningful transformation.

To embark on this path, one can enumerate the imminent changes and explore how each can pave the way for positive outcomes. By adopting a perspective that embraces change as a catalyst for progress, one can effectively adapt and flourish in unfamiliar settings.

Romans 8:28 offers reassurance: *"And we know that all things work together for good to them that love God, to them who are the called according to his purpose."* Trusting that everything happens for a reason and that good can come from even the most challenging situations can help you embrace change with confidence and optimism.

CONCLUSION

Embracing a new identity after divorce involves rediscovering yourself, exploring personal interests, strengthening your faith, building self-confidence, connecting with a supportive community, and embracing change. This journey of self-discovery is a powerful opportunity to grow and thrive. Trust in God's plan for you and allow yourself to evolve into the person you are meant to be.

Reflection Chapter Ten

Q1. Reflect on 2 Corinthians 5:17: "Therefore if any man be in Christ, he is a new creature: old things are passed away; behold, all things are become new." How does this verse inspire you to embrace your new identity after your divorce?

Q2. How have you rediscovered aspects of yourself that you had forgotten or neglected during your marriage?

Q3. What new hobbies or interests have you explored that have helped you understand yourself better?

Q4. Reflect on Galatians 2:20: "I am crucified with Christ: nevertheless, I live; yet not I, but Christ liveth in me: and the life which I now live in the flesh I live by the faith of the Son of God, who loved me and gave himself for me." How does this verse shape your understanding of your identity in Christ?

Q5. How has the process of rediscovering yourself influenced your future goals and aspirations?

Chapter Eleven:

REDISCOVERING JOY AND PURPOSE

Life after divorce can feel like a blank canvas, allowing you to rediscover joy and purpose. While the end of a marriage marks a significant life change, it also provides a unique opportunity to redefine your happiness and set a new course for your life.

Psalm 30:5 reminds us, *"For his anger endureth but a moment; in his favour is life: weeping may endure for a night, but joy cometh in the morning."* This scripture speaks to the hope and renewal that come after a period of sorrow. Embracing this promise can help you look forward to the joy that lies ahead.

EMBRACING NEW OPPORTUNITIES

Divorce can open doors to new opportunities that you may not have considered before. This could mean pursuing a new career, returning to school, or even starting a business. The possibilities are endless, and the key is to stay open to new experiences, empowering you to shape your future as you see fit.

According to a study published in the Journal of Career Development, individuals who experience significant life changes, such as divorce, often find new career opportunities that align more closely with their passions and skills **(Sullivan & Baruch, 2009)**. Embracing these opportunities can lead to a more fulfilling and joyful life.

BUILDING A POSITIVE MINDSET

A positive mindset is crucial for rediscovering joy and purpose. Focusing on the positive aspects of life and maintaining an optimistic outlook can significantly impact your overall happiness and well-being.

Philippians 4:8 advises, "*Finally, brethren, whatsoever things are true, whatsoever things are honest, whatsoever things are just, whatsoever things are pure, whatsoever things are lovely, whatsoever things are of good report; if there be any virtue, and if there be any praise, think on these things.*" By focusing on the good in your life, you can cultivate a positive mindset that fosters joy and contentment.

EXPLORING YOUR PASSIONS

One of the best ways to rediscover joy is by exploring your passions, whether a hobby you once loved or a new interest you have always wanted to try. Engaging in activities that bring you joy can significantly enhance your sense of purpose, giving you the freedom to pursue what truly makes you happy.

Research published in the Journal of Happiness Studies found that individuals who actively engage in hobbies and interests report higher happiness and life satisfaction **(Seligman, 2002).** Dedicating time to what you love can create a more joyful and fulfilling life.

SERVING OTHERS

Finding purpose often involves serving others. Volunteering, mentoring, or helping those in need can bring profound joy and fulfilment, enriching your life in ways you may not have expected.

Matthew 25:40 teaches, *"And the King shall answer and say unto them, Verily I say unto you since ye have done it unto one of the least of these my brethren, ye have done it unto me."* Serving others is a powerful way to connect with your community and find deeper meaning in your life.

RECONNECTING WITH NATURE

Engaging with natural surroundings can be profoundly rejuvenating and inspiring. Whether taking a stroll in a local park, embarking on a mountain hike, or simply finding solace by a serene lake, the tranquil beauty of nature holds a unique ability to revitalize the mind and uplift the spirit.

Psalm 19:1 states, *"The heavens declare the glory of God; and the firmament sheweth his handywork."* Nature reflects the beauty and majesty of God's creation, offering a space for reflection and renewal.

SETTING NEW GOALS

Establishing new objectives provides you with direction and purpose. These objectives can be related to personal growth, career aspirations, health, or any other area you wish to enhance. Accomplishing these objectives can bring a sense of fulfillment and joy.

Proverbs 16:9 says, *"A man's heart deviseth his way: but the Lord directeth his steps."* Setting goals with faith and purpose can lead you toward a more joyful and fulfilling life.

CONCLUSION

Rediscovering joy and purpose after divorce is a journey filled with new opportunities, positive mindset shifts, exploration of passions, service to others, connection with nature, and setting meaningful goals. Embrace this chapter of your life with hope and optimism, trusting in God's plan and the joy ahead.

Reflection Chapter Eleven

Q1. Reflect on Psalm 30:5: "Weeping may endure for a night, but joy cometh in the morning." How does this verse inspire you to seek joy in your new beginnings after divorce?

Q2. What new opportunities have you discovered since your divorce, and how have they contributed to your sense of purpose?

Q3. How can focusing on positive aspects of your life, as suggested in Philippians 4:8, help you maintain a positive mindset and rediscover joy?

Q4. What hobbies or interests have you rekindled or newly explored, and how have they impacted your happiness and fulfillment?

Q5. In what ways can serving others and engaging in acts of kindness bring more joy and purpose into your life?

Chapter Twelve:

CULTIVATING RESILIENCE AND STRENGTH

Resilience, the ability to adapt and recover from adversity, is a crucial trait to cultivate after a divorce. It's about bouncing back from setbacks and growing stronger through your challenges. Building resilience empowers you to navigate the complexities of life after divorce and emerge with a renewed sense of strength and purpose.

James 1:2-4 encourages, *"My brethren, count it all joy when ye fall into divers temptations; Knowing this, that the trying of your faith worketh patience. But let patience have her perfect work, that ye may be perfect and entire, wanting nothing."*This scripture highlights the importance of viewing trials as opportunities for growth and strengthening your faith and resilience.

DEVELOPING COPING STRATEGIES

Building resilience requires effective coping strategies, which can be achieved through mindfulness practices. Deep breathing, yoga, and running are physical exercises that enhance resilience. Furthermore, involvement in creative pursuits such as painting or writing contributes to developing emotional fortitude.

Mindfulness and meditation are crucial in staying grounded and present, reducing anxiety, and promoting emotional balance. A study published in the journal Mindfulness found that mindfulness practices significantly reduce stress and improve emotional regulation **(Hölzel et al., 2011).** Integrating mindfulness into your daily regimen can significantly boost your capacity to handle stress and foster resilience.

BUILDING A SUPPORT NETWORK

Having a solid support network is vital for cultivating resilience. Surrounding yourself with friends, family, and community members who offer emotional support and encouragement and respect your boundaries and needs can significantly improve one's ability to recover from adversity.

Ecclesiastes 4:9-10 states, *"Two are better than one; they have a good reward for their labour. If they fall, the one will lift his fellow: but woe to him that is alone when he falleth; for he hath not another to help him up."* This verse emphasizes the importance of supportive relationships in overcoming challenges.

LEARNING FROM ADVERSITY

Resilience involves learning from adversity and using those lessons to grow stronger. Reflecting on your difficulties and understanding how they have shaped you can provide valuable insights and foster personal growth.

According to a Journal of Personality and Social Psychology study, individuals who reflect on and learn from their adverse experiences tend to develop greater psychological resilience and well-being **(Seery, Holman, & Silver, 2010).** Embracing the lessons learned from your divorce can help you build a stronger, more resilient self.

SETTING BOUNDARIES

Setting boundaries is a critical aspect of building resilience. It involves knowing your limits and protecting your emotional and physical well-being. Setting clear boundaries with your ex-partner, family, and friends is essential. By openly and respectfully communicating your needs and expectations, you can create a safe and supportive environment for healing and personal growth.

Proverbs 25:28 teaches, *"He that hath no rule over his spirit is like a city that is broken down and without walls. "*This verse underscores the importance of self-control and boundaries in maintaining personal strength and resilience.

EMBRACING SELF-COMPASSION

Self-compassion is essential for building resilience and maintaining a positive outlook during difficult times. Being kind to yourself can help you recover quickly from setbacks and keep your spirits high. A study published in Self and Identity found that self-compassion is strongly linked to emotional resilience and psychological well-being **(Neff, Rude, & Kirkpatrick, 2007)**. One can cultivate increased resilience and inner strength by extending to oneself the same compassion and empathy one would readily extend to a friend.

SEEKING PROFESSIONAL HELP

In certain circumstances, enhancing one's resilience may require assistance from trained professionals. Therapists and counsellors possess many valuable tools and strategies to help individuals effectively manage stress and triumph over emotional hurdles. Taking the initiative to seek professional support is not a sign of weakness but rather a proactive and comforting step toward achieving healing and growth.

Matthew 11:28 offers comfort: *"Come unto me, all ye that labour and are heavy laden, and I will give you rest."*This verse reminds us that seeking help, whether spiritual or professional, is vital to finding rest and resilience.

CONCLUSION

Cultivating resilience and strength after divorce is a multifaceted process that involves embracing challenges, developing coping strategies, building a support network, learning from adversity, setting boundaries, practising self-compassion, and seeking professional help. By focusing on these areas, you can grow stronger and more resilient, ready to face the future with confidence and hope.

Reflection Chapter Twelve

Q1. Reflect on James 1:2-4: "My brethren, count it all joy when ye fall into divers temptations; Knowing this, that the trying of your faith worketh patience. But let patience have her perfect work, that ye may be perfect and entire, wanting nothing." How does this verse encourage you to view your challenges as opportunities for growth?

Q2. What new coping strategies have you discovered that help you manage stress and build resilience?

Q3. How has your support network helped you through the difficult times following your divorce? Who are the key people you rely on for support?

Q4. What important lessons have you learned from the adversities you have faced during and after your divorce?

Q5. How can setting clear boundaries help you protect your emotional well-being and foster resilience?

Chapter Thirteen:

A NEW DAWN, A NEW JOURNEY

When undergoing a divorce, individuals often encounter a broad spectrum of emotions, encompassing feelings of grief, relief, guilt, and the prospect of newfound freedom. It is paramount to acknowledge that while divorce may signify the conclusion of a significant chapter, it simultaneously heralds the advent of a new and potentially remarkable journey. This transition period is a time of change and an opportunity for profound personal growth, self-discovery, and embracing fresh prospects and experiences.

EMBRACING A NEW BEGINNING

As you stand on the threshold of this new phase in your life, it is crucial to release guilt, shame, and condemnation. Though natural, these feelings do not define your worth or future.

Reflect on **Isaiah 43:18-19**: *"Remember ye, not the former things, neither consider the things of old. Behold, I will do a new thing; now it shall spring forth; shall ye not know it? I will even make a way in the wilderness and rivers in the desert."* This verse reminds us that God is always at work, creating new pathways and opportunities amid our most challenging times.

FINDING YOUR TRUE SELF

Divorce provides a unique opportunity to rediscover yourself. It's a chance to explore your interests, passions, and dreams that may have been set aside. It's a time to reconnect with your inner self and to find joy in your individuality. Take comfort in knowing that your identity is not solely tied to your marital status but is found in who you are.

Philippians 4:13 encourages us, *"I can do all things through Christ which strengtheneth me."* Draw strength from your faith and from within, knowing that you have the power to overcome and achieve great things. Use this period of transformation to focus on your personal growth and to nurture your emotional and spiritual well-being

BUILDING A FUTURE OF HOPE

The future ahead is filled with possibilities. It is a canvas waiting for you to paint your dreams, aspirations, and hopes. **Jeremiah 29:11** offers reassurance: *"For I know the thoughts that I think toward you, saith the Lord, thoughts of peace, and not of evil, to give you an expected end."* Trust that there is a divine plan for your life, one that is filled with hope and promise.

Engage in activities that genuinely resonate with your passions and bring genuine happiness and a deep sense of fulfillment and purpose. Surround yourself with individuals who uplift and inspire you and challenge and motivate you to become the best version of yourself. Seek a supportive community that encourages personal growth, such as local support groups, online forums, or spiritual communities, and provides the resources and guidance necessary to thrive and achieve your goals. Embrace new experiences with an open mind and heart, and remain receptive to the beauty of unexpected blessings that enrich your life. Remember that each day presents an opportunity to create cherished memories and embrace every moment with gratitude and enthusiasm.

EMBRACING FORGIVENESS AND LETTING GO

Forgiveness is a transformative and healing force that enables us to release resentment and move forward. It involves forgiving ourselves for perceived shortcomings or mistakes and extending compassion to others who may have caused pain. By practising forgiveness, we free ourselves from anger and bitterness, allowing us to embrace peace and emotional well-being. Holding on to resentment only anchors you to the past.

Ephesians 4:31-32 advises, *"Let all bitterness, and wrath, and anger, and clamour, and evil speaking, be put away from you, with all malice: And be ye kind one to another, tenderhearted, forgiving one another, even as God for Christ's sake hath forgiven you."* Embracing forgiveness and letting go means acknowledging the pain, understanding its impact, and choosing to release it, thereby opening your heart to peace and joy.

Letting go of negative emotions opens your heart to peace and joy. It frees you to embrace the future without the weight of the past.

THE JOURNEY AHEAD

The journey ahead is yours to shape. Embrace it with courage and confidence, knowing you are more robust and wiser. Your experiences, though painful, have equipped you with resilience and a deeper understanding of yourself. Celebrate your progress, no matter how small, and continue to strive for the life you envision.

As you embark upon this new phase, you must recognize that you are not navigating this journey in isolation. Many individuals have trodden similar paths and emerged triumphant. Rely on the pillars of your faith, the support of your cherished ones, and the fortitude within you. Remember, you are not alone in this journey, and there are people and resources available to support you.

Divorce is not the end—it is a new beginning. It is the start of a journey that promises renewal, growth, and extraordinary possibilities. Embrace this chapter with hope and anticipation; the best is yet to come. The dawn of a new day awaits, and with it, the opportunity to write a beautiful and fulfilling story. Your future is filled with hope and anticipation, and the best is yet to come.

APPENDIX

Divorcee Experience Questionnaire

Personal Information

1. Age: ______________.   Gender:______________

2. Occupation: ___________________________

3. Length of Marriage: ___________________________

4. Number of Children (if any):_________________

5. How many times have you been married?______

1. What were the main factors that led to your divorce?

____

____

____

____

____

2. What were the most challenging aspects of the divorce, and how did you cope with them?

____

____

____

____

____

3. What are three (3) things you wish you had known before you got married that could have saved your marriage?

____

____

____

____

____

4. Would you consider getting married again? If yes, how do you justify Jesus' teaching in St. Mathew 19? What are three pieces of nuggets you got from your previous marriage that you will take into your next marriage?

____

____

____

____

____

5. How did the divorce impact your financial situation, and what steps did you take to achieve financial independence?

____

____

____

____

____

6. What have you learned about yourself that will help you to become a better version of yourself? (i.e. fulfilling a dream, etc.)

____

____

____

____

____

7. How did you feel during and after the process of telling others about your situation?

____

____

____

____

____

8. What has been your experience with co-parenting (if applicable), and what strategies have been effective?

____

____

____

____

____

9. What advice would you give to persons considering getting divorced or currently going through a divorce?

____

____

____

____

10. Do you think you have made the right decision in getting a divorce?

____

____

____

____

Participant Responses to Divorce Questionnaire.

Demographics

Gender: Female

Age: Above 40

Marital History: Married once

Reasons for Divorce

Participants cited the following reasons for their divorce:

1. Infidelity
2. Emotional abuse
3. Lack of commitment
4. Lack of trust and respect

Challenges Faced

Participants reported facing significant challenges during and after their divorces, including:

1. Humiliation
2. Rejection
3. Abuse
4. Fear

As a result of these challenges, some participants became promiscuous or workaholics.

Pre-Marital Knowledge

Participants expressed a wish they had known the following before getting married:

1. Their own identity
2. How to love themselves
3. How to trust God
4. The importance of spending more time to understand their partner
5. The need to have personal standards and not settle for mediocrity
6. More about their partner's relatives

Attitudes Toward Remarriage
Responses varied about remarriage:

1. Some participants had no plans for immediate remarriage.
2. - Others referenced the Bible, specifically Matthew 19, stating they would consider remarriage if their partner died.

Financial Situation Post-Divorce

Participants, being the household providers, generally did not experience a negative impact on their financial situation. One participant noted an improvement in their life due to relief from the financial burden imposed by their ex.

Lessons Learned

Key lessons learned by participants included:

1. Emotional renewal and realization of being whole and loved by God.
2. Recognizing their worth and deserving of love.
3. Having no regrets about the time invested in the marriage.
4. Focus on the next steps and reflect on the lessons learned from the marriage.

Emotional Impact

Participants expressed feelings of abandonment and loneliness post-divorce. Many had not shared their divorce with close friends and family due to embarrassment. Disclosure about the divorce was described as being on a *"need-to-know basis."*

Co-Parenting

None of the participants co-parented, believing it was the best decision for the children due to **[specific reasons not mentioned]**. If desired, the other party's relationship with the children was not restricted.

Advice to Others

Participants offered the following advice to those considering or going through a divorce:

1. Pray and seek God's guidance before taking action.
2. Seek counselling to ensure that divorce is the best route.
3. Ensure a strong support system.
4. Be happy with the choice you make.

Decision Satisfaction

When asked if they had made the right decision in getting a divorce, all participants responded affirmatively. They viewed it as a new beginning rather than an end, a testament to the potential positive outcomes of such a life-changing decision.

BIBLIOGRAPHY

American Psychological Association. (2020). Building your resilience. Retrieved from https://www.apa.org/topics/resilience

Hölzel, B. K., Carmody, J., Vangel, M., Congleton, C., Yerramsetti, S. M., Gard, T., & Lazar, S. W. (2011). Mindfulness practice leads to increases in regional brain gray matter density. *Psychiatry Research: Neuroimaging, 191*(1), 36-43. doi:10.1016/j.pscychresns.2010.08.006

Mayo Clinic. (2020). Forgiveness: Letting go of grudges and bitterness. Retrieved from https://www.mayoclinic.org/healthy-lifestyle/adult-health/in-depth/forgiveness/art-20047692

Neff, K. D., Rude, S. S., & Kirkpatrick, K. L. (2007). An examination of self-compassion in relation to positive psychological functioning and personality traits. *Self and Identity, 6*(2-3), 224-244. doi:10.1080/15298860601118779

Seligman, M. E. P. (2002). *Authentic happiness: Using the new positive psychology to realize your potential for lasting fulfillment*. New York, NY: Free Press.

Seery, M. D., Holman, E. A., & Silver, R. C. (2010). Whatever does not kill us: Cumulative lifetime adversity, vulnerability, and resilience. *Journal of Personality and Social Psychology, 99*(6), 1025-1041. doi:10.1037/a0021344

Sullivan, S. E., & Baruch, Y. (2009). Advances in career theory and research: A critical review and agenda for future exploration. *Journal of Management, 35*(6), 1542-1571. doi:10.1177/0149206309350082

The Holy Bible, King James Version. (1987). Nashville, TN: Thomas Nelson. (Original work published 1611)

◇◇◇◇◇◇◇◇◇◇◇◇◇◇◇◇◇◇◇◇◇◇◇◇◇◇◇◇◇◇◇◇◇◇◇◇

www.ingramcontent.com/pod-product-compliance
Lightning Source LLC
LaVergne TN
LVHW010606160826
845677LV00013B/3278